THE FEARLESS MONEY MINDSET

BROKE DOESN'T SCARE ME

THE
FEARLESS
MONEY
MINDSET

BROKE DOESN'T SCARE ME

7 Principles for Financial Success

BY ARIAN SIMONE

Hardcover ISBN: 978-1-7348300-0-2

Printed in the United States of America

Cover photography by Dewayne Rogers
Book design by 0514 Design

This book is dedicated to everyone who is

on the journey of their best.

To those who desire

to operate at their highest self.

Table of Contents

Setting
the
Stage

I first started this book off with the introduction which you are about to read—then once I was almost finished with the book, I said, "Arian wait, you need to set the stage." What I mean by that is to provide you with more background info. I thought, *Arian, there are people who are going to read this book and they don't even know who the heck you are. They have no clue of or frame of reference for the stories mentioned.* So, before you read the intro, let me set the stage.

I am Arian Simone, a proud native of Detroit, Michigan with the heart of a hustler. I have been in love with entrepreneurship since I was a child. As my friend Keshia says, I probably came out of the womb selling my mom's placenta. Kay, my best friend Kellie's mom, constantly mentions how I sold poinsettias in middle school to all the parents. My concentration was business at Cass Technical High School and my major at Florida A&M University was business as well. I got a B.S. and an MBA in Florida A&M's five-year program.

While I was in college, I opened my own retail store in the Tallahassee Mall. I remember what it was like to raise capital. While sitting on the store's floor as we prepared for our grand opening, I said, "One day I am going to be the investor who I am looking for." Luckily I remembered that promise, and that is why I am a business investor today.

While owning a store in college, I realized early on that business has its ups and downs. After two years of owning the store, I was done. I wanted to do what everyone else did: go to school, get stellar grades and get a job. In 2003, entrepreneurship was not as popular as it is today. People thought entrepreneurs were crazy, so I set out for what I thought was stability.

I got a job working at Nelly's Apple Bottoms Jeans in Los Angeles. You all know the song *Low* by Flo Rida. Yes, those jeans! In January 2004, I flew to Los Angeles, a city I said I would never live in. But hey, that's where I landed. I was so excited; my job was product placement. I placed products on Jessica Simpson, Tyra Banks, and even Oprah Winfrey. I had a slew of celebrities walking in and out of the office on a regular basis. I was the first in the door to work and the last to leave. I gave my all at any task I was assigned. After 30 days of working there, I was called into the president's office, I just knew I was up for an immediate raise. The president let me know that the company was being sold and that I was to be laid off effective immediately. I was the last hired so I was the first fired. I told myself, "Arian, you are from Detroit. You have plenty of hustle. You will get through this and figure it out."

After a while, my money ran out and I got a notice on my apartment door to pay rent or quit. I had to quit. I packed up my apartment and moved my clothes into the car. My parents were in the midst of their divorce, so it wasn't a good time for them financially either. My mom's best friend Christine paid for my furniture and belongings to be placed in storage. I went from living in an apartment to living out of my car but I was determined to figure things out. I sold my clothes to eat and put gas in the car. I ended up on welfare, food stamps, and general relief—sleeping on a friend's floor and then back to the car. I learned many important lessons during this time, and one of them was to dance in the rain. Despite difficult situations or circumstances, you can still make the choice to enjoy life and have fun, and that's what I did. I ran around LA like a 23 year old would—having fun, sneaking into an award show, parties…you name it.

Don't get me wrong. There is a time when I hit rock bottom and wondered why the heck all this was happening to me. I had applied to more than 153 jobs and no one hired me. I was literally driving my car when I stopped at a green light and could not move. I just had no clue why I couldn't figure out life at that moment. I honestly didn't know where

I was going, so I was going to sit right there at that light until I figured it out.

In that moment, my mom called me and I told her where I was and what I was doing and she freaked out. She said, "You are all the way across the country. You can't do this to me." I let her know that I wasn't suicidal but that I was exhausted. I'd done everything I was told to do but I felt like I was at a dead end. Eventually, I did move the car, because if I would have sat there any longer I may have gotten arrested.

Months after being let go from Apple Bottoms, someone called who'd noticed my work there and sought me out to do public relations and marketing independently.

Although I'd never specifically done that type of work before, I knew it was my shot. Whenever someone gives me a door, I don't walk through it—I run through it. The people who called me then referred me to other people who referred me to other people. I looked up and I had a full-on business in a matter of two weeks with five to seven clients.

I called my line sister Catarah (who you will read about later) and I asked her to move to Los Angeles the following year to help me with the company since she was a PR major. Over some years, the PR company grew very fast.

It had ups and downs like any business. But unlike with the store, I knew that came with doing business.

At age 21, with the retail store's ups and downs I kept thinking I was failing so I left it alone. Looking back now, I realized that I wasn't failing. I simply lacked patience. I realized that if business was what I was supposed to do, I would just have to ride the wave and all would be okay. I also realized that working for someone else wasn't aligning with the stars. Heck, I'd applied to more than 153 jobs. If working for someone else was what I was supposed to do then one of those doors should have opened.

The PR and marketing business had clients from Sony Pictures, Universal, Walt Disney and almost every major Hollywood studio. We provided PR and marketing services for films such as *Ride Along*, *Takers*, *Hancock*, *Limitless*, *James Bond 007*: *Quantum of Solace* and a host of others. We serviced chart topping music artists, executed extravagant events and more.

Over time, I realized that one of the ingredients to my success was my fearlessness and I wanted the world to have it. I wanted everyone to know they can live whatever dreams they may have. I started the *Fearless* platform in 2010 and here we are with a brand arm, venture arm and philanthropic arm.

Now that I have provided some context as to why broke doesn't scare me and why I know abundance is available, let's get into this book!

Introduction

Picture this: it's 2006 on a cool evening in Los Angeles. The breeze sifts through the palm trees and I'm in the driver's seat of my new gold Cadillac CTS at the drive-thru at El Pollo Loco. My line sister Catarah Hampshire (now Coleman) is in the passenger seat. As I wait for the cashier to bag my food, I glance over at Catarah who looks at me and says, "See, it happened again."

I replied with curiosity, "What happened again?"

"It happened again, your faith is unwavering," she responded.

I was flattered but still somewhat curious as to what she meant so I asked her again. She said, "Arian, this morning you said that you needed $10,000 by 4pm, and it happened."

As she brought it to my attention, I was reminded of how God had always met me at my level of faith and expectancy. I took a brief moment to reflect and my response to her was simple. I said, "Well yes, of course." She went on to tell me again how my faith was unwavering and how she had witnessed me go into things sometimes blindly, and how ultimately things always tended to work out for me. I let her know being broke doesn't scare me so I don't place my energy there. I place my energy in my faith in receiving abundance.

As I graciously took in what my good friend Catarah said, I began to think back on how favor had always seemed to follow me. The favor that I experienced and that others were able to witness was a result of me being convinced that God moves on my behalf. Most people fall short on their goals because they rely too heavily on logic, when in fact, building anything extraordinary—or achieving something remarkable—requires a certain level of risk and unrelenting faith. These key elements are the components of fearlessness.

Now don't get me wrong. You do need logic. You do need hard work. But it requires courage to create a life that reflects your heart's desires. No one ever achieved greatness by succumbing to their fears. It's not that fear doesn't show up; what matters more is the ability to go forth despite any angst that may be present. You see, fear is just an illusion; a negative idea that shows up to keep you playing, believing, thinking and dreaming small.

My conversation with my friend Catarah is so profound to me today. At that time I didn't fully process the totality of how my life journey was really a faith walk matched with a whole lot of work and heart. During that car ride, I had listened to everything that she said, but her point didn't really sink in until years later. If I believed something was going to happen for me, I refused to entertain any thoughts that would counter what I believed.

Our beliefs influence our behavior. When you truly believe that something is possible, your daily actions align with that belief. If you are making a decision solely based upon what you can see then you are not allowing any room for greater possibilities. You are limiting your potential and you aren't leaving any room for your faith to be activated.

I actually understand Catarah's perspective in large part now because if we're not careful, the world can condition us to operate more from a standpoint of fear than faith. Fear works overtime to prevent us from experiencing anything outside of our realm of comfort. Fear kicks in to keep us from doing anything that involves any risk. The truth of the matter is that our comfort zones don't keep us safe; they keep us small.

I am reminded of my conversation with Catarah whenever I'm faced with any doubt. I reflect on her words as she described me in action. When I think back on how my fearlessness has been the catalyst for so many opportunities in my life, any reservations I feel when facing a new goal or even a new challenge quickly subsides. That candid conversation with Catarah affirmed just how powerful my faith and action had been throughout my journey. It was a riveting reminder of how taking action in the direction of my dreams is a reflection of me in my most authentic form.

That type of fearlessness resides in each of us.

Jasena, my girlfriend's daughter who is like a niece to me, once asked me to explain to a young child what being fearless meant. At first, I declined the offer, but after being asked a second time I obliged. I was asked, "Arian, break this concept of fearlessness down so that even a young child can understand what it means." I was being charged to simplify and articulate something that to me was already so simple. I finally responded and said, "I don't have to tell a child anything about being fearless because they already are!"

A child between the ages of one and five years old are the most fearless and honest human beings you will encounter. They will jump into a pool whether they know how to swim or not! Their imaginations run wild. They are creative and they don't have any limitations. Fear is a learned behavior. It isn't until someone is taught to fear something that they actually do. It's no one's original or natural state of being. God didn't give us the spirit of fear but He gave us power, love and a sound mind. We did not come here with any fear; fear is something that we learned and after we adopted fear, it became a behavior.

My nephew Carter is five years old with a caramel complexion, sandy brown curly hair, and big, bright brown eyes. Carter is my best friend Kellie's son and he affectionately calls me Auntie Arian (both of her boys do). Carter stood proudly at his pre-kindergarten graduation when his teacher asked him what he wanted to be when he grew up. He boldly replied, "I am going to be a superhero!"

See, this is what I am talking about. The adults probably thought, *Someone please help this child.* I even went to my best friend Kellie and said, "Did you hear what Carter said? What's your response?"

Kellie said, "I told him that he could be a superhero at anything he wanted to be a superhero at."

I loved how she kept his imagination where it was, but lovingly guided his larger-than- life enthusiasm with purpose and direction. She didn't crush his creativity by telling him that being a superhero was not feasible or attainable. For the record, both of Kellie's kids, Chase and Carter are off-the-chart geniuses. No, I am not saying this because I am a proud Aunt. I am serious!

Carter was learning and reciting geometry at age two, and Chase, his older brother builds robots that your average teenager couldn't complete. One day I walked into the house and saw both Carter at age three and Chase at age seven playing chess. They offered to teach me how to play and I darn near fell out. Kellie picked up on my astonishment and assured me that the boys really did know what they were talking about. I am glad that she was able to vouch for them because I never learned how to play chess, but I did know the object of the game. Had she not said anything, I wouldn't have known whether they were teaching me checkers, chess, or Connect 4.

One day when Carter lost a tooth, he said to me, "Auntie Arian, look I got a dollar from the tooth fairy."

"Carter keep saving your dollars, you're going to be rich," I said.

He looked at me sternly and said, "Going to be? I AM RICH."

I said, "Yes, baby you are rich."

He interjected and continued affirming himself. "I AM RICH, I AM SMART, I AM HANDSOME, I AM TALENTED." He went on and on. See, the kids know exactly who they are. They come into this world limitless.

Now, here we are as adults afraid to take a chance that could change our lives, afraid to build something that fulfills us, afraid to walk away from things that no longer serve us. We have to get back to that place of pure ambition and begin to apply our wisdom to their childlike innocence and fearlessness.

The reason that I started the book off talking about kids is because it's a great example of how we come equipped into the world. We come here with confidence. We are born bold. We start off with courage and dedication for what we want. Think about a baby who wants your phone. That child will do whatever it takes to get you to give in to what they want, whether they scream until your ears can't take it, or ask you over and over and over until you finally cave. Children operate out of instinct and commitment to what they want. Anything opposite of that has been learned from our societal constructs, family function, past disappointment or environment.

In the middle of filming a commercial for Ford's digital campaign entitled "Sisterhood of Boss Women." The campaign included myself, costume designer June Ambrose, entrepreneur Claire Sulmers, and magazine editor Amy Dubois Barnett.

While on set, June looked at me and said, "What is special about you? What is the light that you have?" She looked at me intently again and said, "No, really, what is it?"

I don't recall what I said at the time but I later went back and thought about it more and realized that I had maintained some of those childlike characteristics of believing anything was possible. Clearly, she had as well. By the looks of June's social media pages, she constantly creates, and dances like no one is watching, while living a colorfully-adventurous life.

We all come from different socioeconomic backgrounds, and time and again it is proven that whether you grew up rich or poor, wealth is available to you. There are so many stories of people growing up in poverty and becoming rich or wealthy. Now this is not to make light of any of the systemic foolishness that exists in trying to keep minorities in certain places; what this book offers is principles you can apply to win despite any situation or circumstance.

Fear is the root of a "lack energy." As I've traveled around the world, coaching, speaking with, training, mentoring and inspiring people from all walks of life, all socioeconomic backgrounds and various religious upbringings, the one commonality across the board was the fear at the core of every manifestation of lack.

It is fear that causes people to continue to clock in day in and day out at a job that pays them just enough to pay their revolving bills. It's this same fear that makes them feel that anything outside of their everyday routine is pointless. When I see people bypass great opportunities and settle for good enough, it's always because they don't truly believe in themselves or the power that they possess. This limited belief system is what fuels the construct of poverty.

Poverty by definition is not having enough material possessions or income for a person's needs. Poverty can include social, economic and political elements. While I'm very aware of the societal injustices and global trends that contribute most to the disparaging prevalence of lack, it is the mindset of individuals that keeps them from breaking free from the bondage of scarcity. This does not take away systemic issues that need to be removed. Justice still needs to prevail, but we all can overcome.

Working with so many ambitious people who were full of creativity but lacked capital really compelled me to focus on developing resources that would equip them with the necessary tools to truly experience financial freedom. What I realized was that most people didn't have a finance problem but rather an issue with fear. These individuals possessed the kind of creative and witty ideas that Fortune 500 companies generate millions in revenue from. But without access, knowledge and the right mindset, those ideas continue to be a best-kept secret.

One reason I wrote this book is because there are way too many talented individuals who are full of ideas but are restricted by their own fears. I made it my business to complete this manuscript because far too many people have self-sabotaging beliefs about money. The worst part of all is that many of them don't even realize how their mindset is messing up their money. People have so many fears around the subject of money that it is overwhelming.

I wrote this book to help eradicate those fears so that men and women worldwide could upgrade their mindset, rid themselves of life-limiting fears and adopt a fearless framework that would allow them to increase their finances. The common fears and mental limitations about money are:

1. **The fear of living paycheck to paycheck**

2. **The fear of not being able to secure a future**

3. **The fear of failing**

4. **The fear of becoming a target**

5. **The fear of not having enough**

6. **The fear of revisiting a past financial trauma**

7. **The fear of trusting a financial professional**

This book offers viable solutions to help you overcome these fears so that you can adopt a *Fearless Money Mindset.* This book is a fearless guide to help you achieve financial success. The seven principles outlined in this book eliminate the above fears and have personally helped me to make, manage and maximize my money.

You picked up this book because you are a fearless go-getter with a vision for greatness and you're tired of being your own worst enemy. Or maybe you have mastered the art of attracting money but you continue to come up short because you are able to make money, but struggle to manage it.

Perhaps you're a dreamer with a vision, but because you feel as though you don't have the resources to achieve your goals, you've settled for what was sure; and day in and day out you live with gut-wrenching guilt and the recurring feeling of regret. You've put your faith on the back burner and you've allowed your fears to take the driver's seat, and now you're finally ready to kick fear to the curb so that you can experience the personal fulfillment of achieving greatness.

Or maybe you're already making seven figures and you find yourself still living beneath your potential. You know there is so much more in store for you. You are what society would call successful. You have a nice family, big home, nice cars, and you vacation but your yearning to be more is ever so strong. While you have plenty of money in your bank account, you know you are still not at your best and highest self. That questionable emotion that revisits you is a call for you to dig deeper and to go higher. The recurring thought that compels you to question if there is more within you is perhaps a personal petition for you to discover that you are only scratching the surface of your limitless potential.

This book is about removing those fears so that you can develop a mindset that allows you to make your money work for you. These seven principles are designed to help you experience financial freedom and authentic fulfillment.

Whether you want to make millions, live comfortably, or buy a large corporate building—whatever your financial goals are—it's all possible once you walk in your power and remove the barriers. You have the power to set your income, dictate your revenue, establish your net worth and achieve massive goals. This is about getting you in the right mindset to take fearless action in the direction of your dreams. This book was written with you in mind.

Chapter 1
The Belief Principle

A mind is a terrible thing to waste

We have heard a thousand times that a mind is a terrible thing to waste because it is. Mindset is so underrated and really needs to be given more attention. A *Fearless Money Mindset* is really a faith mindset. By default, you are always going to believe in something because literally everyone believes in something.

I was traveling abroad in Cuba when this guy asked me about my faith. I responded with enthusiasm and told him that I was Christian. He told me that he didn't believe in anything. I assured him that he did, in fact, believe in something because believing in nothing is still a belief system. He told me that he was an atheist and believed that there was no God. After letting him communicate why he didn't believe in anything, I urged him to reflect on his last statement: "I believe that there is no God." I encouraged him to take inventory of his statement; the very first two words declared that, in fact, he "believed." Although he didn't share my set of beliefs, I wanted him to recognize that even believing in the idea that there is no God, was still indicative of a belief system. With astonishment, he said, "Oh gosh, you're right."

There are times that you will hear someone say, "Oh, I am not making a decision on that." What they often fail to realize is that even when opting not to make a decision, they were still making a decision. They were deciding not to decide. You see? Everyone believes in something, and it is our beliefs that influence our decisions.

In May of 2009, I drove cross country from Los Angeles to Tallahassee, Florida in 38 hours. (I slept for two hours in Houston at a younger sorority sister's house). I drove down in a silver 2006 Mercedes CLS 500. I planned on spending the summer in Tallahassee and taking business education courses at Florida A&M University. This was one of the few times where I thought I could escape entrepreneurship. The economy had taken a hit and I thought I could just take a break. But when you are called to do great things, you start getting nudges that push you to do more.

I'd decided to get a teacher's certificate that I would use to teach students. Instead of getting a certificate, however, I ended up building a program—a full-on curriculum that was actually purchased by the schools and funded by Title I.

On the first day of the teacher certification program, I entered my psychology class which was a large room with stadium seating. The instructor, a light-brown-skinned woman about 5´5 in height, stood at the bottom of the classroom. She sported long dreads and was passionate about teaching the importance of holistic living. This particular day she asked the class, "If I gave a math test right now, raise your hand if you believe that you are going to do well." Keep in mind that this was a psychology class so I wondered where she was going with this.

I, along with eight other students, raised my hand. It was a class of more than 100 students. I looked around in shock that there were not more hands raised—but some may have been thrown off because again this was a psychology class. The professor eased our confusion when she went on to explain that the nine students with their hands raised represented the percentage of students who would go on and do well. I was a bit perplexed, but she explained that the students who raised their hands subconsciously possessed a belief that they had the ability to do well even in an unexpected situation. Those of us who believed we could, most likely would.

She began her lecture on efficacy—a word I wasn't familiar with until that day. Efficacy is defined as "the ability to produce a desired result." As the professor elaborated, when you go into something knowing that you will do well at it, you increase your chances for success. As I built my curriculum, I realized that I first had to get the students in the program to believe! I'd seen during that first psychology class the power of belief and how belief produces results.

Too many thoughts surrounding money are derived from a lack of belief. In order to change your financial outcome, you must first believe that you can. You have to establish a healthy relationship with money that is grounded in a positive convinced belief.

My cousin Candace—middle-aged, gorgeous, and known in the family for her wisdom and humor—looked at one of the toddlers running around at our cousin Laila Simone's ninth birthday party.

"Look at him. I want to be like that," Candace said. "He doesn't have a worry in the world at all. He is not concerned about how the lights will get paid. He just knows that when he flips the light switch on, there will be light." She went on to explain how she'd like to model her life in a worry-free manner.

To Candace's point, that child knows no different until someone tells him something different. I continue to reference children because if you can return to that state of freedom while applying the wisdom that you've earned and developed today, then you can reduce stress and anxiety in your life while increasing fulfillment and freedom.

I challenge you to write down all the traits a child between the ages of one and five possesses. Next, I want you to reflect on the time in your life when you were able to embrace the freedom of your childhood. Understand that you still have that liberated imagination, creativity and fearless ambition. It's still in you; you have to awaken the child within.

CHILDLIKE TRAITS YOU
WISH TO RECLAIM

1.

2.

3.

4.

5.

Naivete

There is a level of power in naivete!

I can remember working with film producer Will Packer on set while he was being interviewed. Someone asked him how he became a big movie producer at such a young age. He responded by sharing some milestones in his journey before stating, "There is a level of power in naivete." He continued by explaining that he didn't know or have the belief that what he was doing was indeed difficult and therefore never adopted the mindset that anything he pursued was beyond his scope of potential. He never felt as if he was unable, or incapable of achieving great things. The fear of failure was not able to limit him in that way.

This is why it's so important to be mindful about who you have in your ear. No one knows anything is difficult until someone tells them that it is. If you adopt the belief that something is difficult then it will be. Again, you are going to believe in something, but you get to choose what that is. Your belief then is not only a choice but the foundation of your behavior. Your beliefs dictate how you behave. The ideas you hold directly impact the actions you take.

At the age of 24, I was stopped by someone in my field who said, "Wow! You sure did crack the glass ceiling."

"What ceiling," I asked.

46

"You are working on films and getting movie studio contracts at 24," she replied.

I didn't know a ceiling even existed—and in reality, it doesn't. It only existed in her mind and anyone's mind who adopts that mentality.

Again, you always believe in something, but if you don't know something exists you cannot believe in it. Now, this does work both ways. If someone doesn't know something positive exists, how are they going to believe in it too?

The Mind of a Winner

I want to pause and reflect on a very popular story. Regardless of our faith, we have all heard of the story of David and Goliath. We use this story and analogy to describe many things that happen in everyday life. One day I heard businesswoman and pastor Sarah Jakes Roberts say we look at David as an underdog but he is really a front runner. This statement prompted me to re-read this story and look at it from David's perspective. We usually tell this story from the viewpoint of the people who have told it to us. All too often, when we hear a story repeatedly, we start to take on the perspective of the person telling the story instead of looking at the story from all possible angles. When I re-read the story from David's vantage point, I saw how he never believed that he was an underdog. In his mind, he was always the champion.

For starters, David volunteered to fight Goliath. He wasn't asked or summoned. He flat out wanted to fight a giant. He viewed Goliath no differently than the bear and lion he had killed in the field while tending to the sheep. He basically said, "Hmm, check my track record. This is light work!"

We know how the story ends. David takes Goliath down with a sling and a stone. David never once got nervous. He didn't look at Goliath and say, "Oh gosh, what have I gotten myself, into?" He was convinced of his victory before he entered the battle. David was unwavering in his belief that he could take Goliath out.

To anyone witnessing it, David was out his mind. There are some things you may attempt to do and people will be on the sidelines thinking you are out of your mind. Just like David, let them witness. Everyone isn't called to prophesy. Some people are called to witness. Let them watch.

I saw a similar scenario play out in a football game. I love watching sports. It was Super Bowl LI in 2017 for the 2016 season: the Atlanta Falcons versus the New England Patriots. I was at my best friend Kellie's house watching the game with her family. Everyone in the house was rooting for the Falcons. I have never cared for the Patriots ever—and I mean ever. I cheered for whoever played against them so I cheered for and with Atlanta. I was glad to root for the Falcons considering that Atlanta is where I presently live.

The game started off with much excitement. Atlanta was winning 7-0, then 14-0, then 21-0. The house was screaming. All of Atlanta was excited. Then toward the end of the first half, the Patriot's scored three points with a field goal and I was like *oh no.*

"Girl, it's just three points. We still have this," Kellie said.

"I am not saying 'oh no' because of the three points," I said. "I'm saying 'oh no' because the Patriots are rejoicing about the three points. This isn't good."

"Arian, it will be fine," Kellie said.

"I don't know that for sure," I replied. "There is something powerful about rejoicing over three points after being down by 21 points. They are not defeated in their minds and that is the most powerful thing to have on the field: not muscles but mindset."

Who in their right mind rejoices over three points after being down by 21? Champions do. Because these Patriots had seen victory before, they knew victory was possible again—just like David with the bear and lion.

The game continued after the half with Atlanta scoring to take the game to a 28-3 lead.

"See," Kellie said.

"Look at them," I said pointing to the Patriots. "They don't look defeated. They are cool, calm, and collected. Anyone down by 25 points in the second half of a game is usually concerned. By now, we should see someone cussing someone out."

The Patriot's calm state had me in complete concern. I knew what it was—it was their unwavering mindset and that was nothing to play with. We continued to watch the game and the Patriots managed to score. It was a 28-9 game, then 28-12, then 28-20, then 28-28. At that point, I looked at Kellie.

I said, "Girl, I told you at 21-3 when the Patriots were jumping up and down and chest bumping that this was about to be a problem. Now it's 28-28 overtime." The Patriots ended up winning the Super Bowl with a score of 34-28.

If you're a sports fan, then you know how emotional sports can be. Yes, I was upset but I recognized the mind of a champion and I hope all who watched were able to take that away from the game. When you enter into something with an unwavering spirit and a convinced mindset, the results are limitless!

The Shift in Belief

Hebrews 10:35-36 says, "Do not throw away your confidence; it will be richly rewarded." If I am being warned to not throw something away, that means that I already have it in my possession. I cannot throw away something that I do not already own. I cannot tell you to toss away your purple bag if you don't have a purple bag. If I say, "Hey, hand me your sandwich," that means that I see a sandwich in your hand and you are able to hand it to me. That sandwich is in your possession. When the Bible tells us to not throw away our confidence that means it was ours to start with. You already have it; just don't throw it away. The Bible goes on to say that we should keep it because it has a rich reward.

When you are convinced—and I mean really convinced—of something it manifests on your behalf. Everyone loves to hear me tell the story about sneaking into the BET Awards. (Pick up my previous books, *My Fabulous & Fearless Journey* and *Fearless Faith + Hustle* if you don't know the story.) I was convinced that I would be granted access and that's how I got it in. I believe in the principle of "acting as if it's already done." I applied some works with my faith, dressed the part and got myself down to the event. My mindset was this: I was confident in the outcome. My belief in what was possible was unwavering!

I started this book with the belief principle because what happens in our minds is the vehicle that manifests what we experience in our worlds. Bold belief is a success tool that transcends gender gaps, ethnic disparities and socio-economic boundaries. Having a healthy mindset is critical—whether you are born into money, or you're a first-generation millionaire.

Our mindset is underrated. We're so much more powerful

than we give ourselves credit for. The truth of the matter is that so many people are operating at a limited version of themselves. I want to drop a pin there. I once thought I was doing great because of the praise I received on social media. People on social media don't know what your best is so they are cheering for everything that you do whether it's your personal best or not. The continuous accolades can have you thinking you are doing just fine. But you may need to take a week or two off of social media and ask yourself are you truly being your best. If there was no applause, is this what you would produce?

No matter how successful you believe you are, how much money you've made, or how much success you've acquired, as long as you're still breathing, there's a greater version of you waiting on the horizon to be birthed from your willingness to take inspired action.

Whether you've made $800,000 this year or $8,000, employing a belief principle that allows you to confidently and boldly commit to growth will always be in your favor. No one ever regrets getting better. The question at hand is both personal and powerful. You must ask yourself, what is the highest version of myself? What does my life look like when I activate my best effort consistently? What behaviors, beliefs and practices do I need to adopt in order to activate my best self?

Contrary to popular belief, limiting beliefs are not reserved for the poor. There are plenty of individuals with money, assets and wealth who are successful but still merely scratching the surface of what is possible for them.

Can you imagine that? That is an indicator of just how powerful we are. Whether you are at the height of your career, or you find yourself in a tight spot, the good news is that there is still more available to you. There is still an abundance of growth and resources available to you.

This is why it's so important to surround yourself with those who have committed to being lifelong learners. The more you learn, the more you earn and the more you evolve. The danger of being in proximity to mediocrity is the illusion of greatness. When you are in an environment where you are the smartest or most successful, the applause and admiration could trick you into believing that you have reached your peak when in reality you may not be doing enough. Your close relationships often work as a tool to forecast how far you will go in life. This is why it is so critical to always abandon your comfort zone. You have heard the saying before: *If I'm the smartest person in the room, then I'm in the wrong room.* When you surround yourself with those who are further ahead, you expand your potential to learn.

Having this sort of awareness is a part of abundant thinking. No matter where you find yourself in relation to your goals, there will always be room to grow. The thing about mindset is that if we are in tune with ourselves, we will always receive some sort of inkling that it's time to move on, learn more or take another step forward—or even in another direction. You'll know when it's time to adjust your thinking when you begin to notice lack.

When you begin to recognize deficiencies, this is often an indicator that your focus has shifted from abundance. Work daily to focus more on the possibilities in your life rather than the problems and potential challenges. A winner only sees the finish line, while others get distracted by hurdles, people on the sidelines and other individuals in the race. Focus on what you want to achieve and eliminate anything that takes away from that. If you want to achieve financial freedom and adopt a *Fearless Money Mindset*, then you must focus on HOW you will manifest these things in your life rather than all the reasons why you can't or the difficulties you may experience in the process. What you focus on will expand, so be sure to divert your attention toward the outcome you desire.

When we begin to work on eliminating the fears around money I want you to explore the highest version of yourself. Remember, it's not a dollar amount, it's about maximum potential.

Adopting a *Fearless Money Mindset* requires a level of confidence. You must be fortified in your beliefs and then make informed financial decisions. If there is a dollar amount you are looking to achieve, are you confident about the amount you want? Do you believe that it's already yours?

Here is the SHIFT! We already know by default and the examples provided above that we are going to believe in something. It's just our natural state of being; it's simply how all humans are wired.

Financial freedom, wealth, abundance and all of these things exist because you have witnessed these things in the lives of others, or maybe you've experienced them in your own life. The question is, do you believe all of this is possible for you? It is easy to believe in what you can see or what you have experienced, the challenge is holding belief for something that has not happened yet. Can you believe that abundance is your birthright, although you may have been born into poverty? Can you believe that you can earn a million dollars although your company may have just taken a hit?

No matter where you find yourself in the realm of possibilities, you must maintain belief and enthusiasm in what is possible, and the truth is that it's all possible. All of your dreams, financial goals and ambitions are all possible. Here is what we choose to believe in so that we have a healthy relationship with money:

FEARLESS MONEY MINDSET BELIEFS

1. We believe that money is a tool that gives us access.

2. We believe that there is an abundance of money, and that there is more than enough money for everyone. *(Last time I checked, the United States Department of the Treasury prints money daily.)*

3. We believe that money always flows towards us easily and effortlessly.

4. We believe that unexpected money always finds its way to us.

5. We believe that money is attracted to us and our purpose.

6. We believe that money provides us with the freedom to make choices.

7. We believe that with more money, we can help more people.

This is the longest of the seven chapters and principles—not because its first but because it's so foundational for the next six. It is truly the base to build from.

Chapter 2
The Thought Principle

Change your thoughts and

you can change your world

Lawd!!! When I became aware that thoughts become reality, I knew then that I had to take control of any thoughts I entertained. It's impossible to think good thoughts and feel bad at the same time—much like it's impossible to think bad thoughts and expect to feel good. Thinking good thoughts and feeling well are of top priority when it comes to improving your mindset around money and anything else for that matter.

If someone could transcribe all of your thoughts on paper, what would your thoughts spell out? Are your thoughts filled with problems and stressors? Are you worried about how a bill is going to get paid? Are you thinking about a lack of finances? Are your thoughts rooted in poverty?

Again, thoughts become reality; if your thoughts are focused on all the things that keep you stuck; you can pretty much count on staying where you are. The world you entertain in your mind will be the life you continue to manifest physically.

What you focus on is what expands in your life. If you focus on negative thoughts, then you will attract and manifest more negativity. If you focus on positive thoughts then you will attract more positive experiences. Whatever you think about, you will notice more of.

Have you ever noticed how after you purchase a new car, you see the same car everywhere? Everywhere you go you notice someone who drives the same car as you. You notice it on the highway, in the mall parking lot, on television, and even in magazines. It's not that more people have the same car as you. It's just that now that you have it, and it has become familiar to you, you now recognize it more often.

The same is true of other thoughts with which you've become familiar. When you rehearse the same self-sabotaging thoughts, you set yourself up to see more of it in your life. Because you may have become so used to lack, you tend to see it everywhere because it is familiar.

Having a *Fearless Money Mindset* allows you to take control of your mind by choosing better thoughts. If you believe that you are not capable of generating millions of dollars in revenue then you most likely won't take any of the necessary actions that will put you in a position to earn or attract multiple figures. In fact, if you don't literally change your mind about money, you most likely won't earn any more than what you are currently making. Like most things in life, if you want to change the outcome then you have to change the action.

If you want to see an increase in your earning potential, then there has to be a shift in the way you think and behave when it comes to money.

> **FEARLESS FACT:**
> *48% of individuals surveyed report that they could not come up with $2000 if an unexpected need arose within 30 days.*

That's nearly half of the people who were surveyed. I'm willing to bet that the main reason why such a large number of these individuals are unable to come up with the money is because they don't think they can.

When you adopt a *Fearless Money Mindset*, you don't settle for thoughts and ideas about why you are unable to achieve a certain outcome. Instead, you work to figure out how you can do it. It's so much more effective and even empowering when you counter your needs and challenges with solutions and strategies.

In order to transform your money mindset, you will first need to train your thoughts. The first step is to acknowledge that it is possible to come up with any amount you choose.

The next step is to know it will be easy to receive it. The third, of course, is to set a plan in motion. You must trade in any limiting beliefs keeping you trapped in the same old currency-capping cycle for thoughts that will bring about outcomes that are both positive and profitable.

Disrupting undesirable thought cycles will allow you to think and live differently. The key is to become familiar with a new set of thoughts. Incorporating a positive statement or a powerful slogan that affirms and also aligns with your upgraded set of beliefs will prove to be very effective. I like to call these sacred utterances *Fearless Money Mantras.*

Since increasing your value and maximizing your earning potential is not just about how hard you work, you must improve the virtue of your beliefs and make a deliberate effort to think well. People are working hard right now doing slave labor and not earning much, so it's clear that the mental and the physical must align for your desired outcome. When your thoughts are wealthy, you will manifest riches in your life.

I remember listening to an audio training by entrepreneur and motivational speaker Jim Rohn. On it, he spoke about wealth and the disparities among income groups. I recall having an "aha" moment when he asserted that even if we split all of the money in the world up and distributed it evenly among everyone, eventually all of the wealth would end up back into the same hands.

This argument is based on the idea that rich people are rich because they think and behave differently. Now, there are some institutional and systemic structures that greatly contribute to the low socioeconomic conditions of certain demographics, but for the sake of this argument the wealth of the world would end up in the same hands because those who are rich understand and engage in wealth-generating activities. Not only do they use their time to produce, sale and distribute; they have a mindset that is fortified in the belief that money is available to them.

When your belief system is based in abundance, you can attract, earn, generate and manifest plenty. What you visualize has a very large impact on what you think about. I have said in my previous book, *Fearless Faith + Hustle* that you will materialize what you visualize. This is because when you see something, it then impacts your thoughts. This is why it's important to monitor what you allow your children to watch on television and other mobile devices. What you entertain is what remains. The word "entertain" by definition means "to give attention or consideration to an idea, suggestion or feeling."

When you give your attention to something, you are then tuning into and subscribing to that idea. Are there some ideas, behaviors and beliefs to which you may need to unsubscribe? Take this quick fearless assessment to measure your money mindset.

MONEY MINDSET QUESTIONNAIRE

If you believe that time creates money, you'll always think you have to trade your time for money. However, if you believe that value creates money, you'll focus on providing so much value to the world without thinking about time. This small difference is everything for creating wealth. Answer the questions below to identify and change what your current money beliefs are.

1. Do you currently exchange your time for money?

2. What do you believe about saving and having money? Do you currently have a systematic way

to save? Do you have a minimum standard for what you keep in your checking account?

3. What do you believe about debt? Do you think that there is good debt and bad debt?

4.   How do you feel when you spend money? Are your spending habits the result of an addictive trait or would you say that you have a more controlled approach to your spending?

5. What do you believe about rich people? Poor people?

6. Are you open to receiving money?

7. What has your past experience been with money? Do you allow past negative experiences to govern your narrative regarding money?

8. What were you taught about money growing up (saving, investing, debt, earning, etc.)?

I want you to assess your current thoughts about money to see if they are lack-focused or abundance-focused, disciplined-focus or just going with the wind. If you notice something in the above answers that you do not like, come up with a plan to counter it so you can begin the process to adjust your beliefs, thoughts, and actions. It is so important to have self-awareness as you navigate through life. You have to be honest with yourself and know where you are in order to go to the next level.

When Catarah and I were in the early years of our PR and marketing company, we met with celebrities who sometimes did not have a clear assessment of where they were in the marketplace. If they seemed to be delusional about this, we didn't take them on. It's not that they couldn't grow into or reach where they thought they were. We are not ones to crush anyone's dreams and we want everyone to live their best life. However, when these individuals didn't have a clear vision of their position in the marketplace, it was harder to get them there. We've even had people come back to us later and confirm that we were right.

I mentioned previously about being mindful of what our children watch. While we are on the subject of thoughts, I have a couple stories I would like to share. Like most people I know, I was obsessed with *the Cosby Show* while growing up. We had every episode on VHS. Yes! We had over 200 episodes in our video catalog. We also had the legendary and iconic show *A Different World* on tape. Of course, being a brown girl growing up in the 80s with long thick hair, everyone would say, "Oh, you remind me of Rudy Huxtable."

Well fast-forward, Keshia Knight Pulliam (the actress who portrayed the character Rudy Huxtable in *the Cosby Show)* and I met right after college and we became fast friends. Now she is one of my closet friends and also one of my business partners.

About 10 years into our friendship, I said, "Keshia, I think I manifested you."

She said, "How?"

"I know everyone claims they watched *the Cosby Show*," I replied. "But for me, this thing was serious. Like, I re-watched those VHS tapes heavily after we recorded the show. In my mind, you were my friend and now here you are my friend in real life."

I know to most this may sound silly but I spent so much time imagining this and then look what happened. I can give you another example.

In college there was a rap artist I had a crush on. Even my little sister called me one day and said, "Arian, this guy I am looking at on television in this music video is so your type." We giggled at the thought of it. I had never met him in my life. But somehow I already had an inkling as to who my sister was talking about. Fast forward ahead a month or even less, I was flying back to Tallahassee, Florida from Las Vegas. During that time, I owned a store in the mall while I attended Florida A & M University as an undergrad. I took trips to MAGIC Trade Show Las Vegas where I purchased inventory for my boutique, connected with other designers and creatives, and learned about new industry trends.

When I landed in Tallahassee, I hopped in my 1999 white Audi and turned on the radio. When I turned on the radio, the rap artist who I had a crush on—the same guy my sister saw on television—announced that he was heading to my store in the mall for his promo tour. We didn't have any events planned or booked with him. I didn't even know he was in Tallahassee. I didn't even know him. I had never met him in person or spoken to him on the phone. He was a complete stranger.

He showed up to my store for what he claimed was a stop that was a part of his tour. But neither my staff nor I knew anything about it. I did not look my best. I'd literally just hopped off of a four-and-a-half-hour flight. My hair was in a bun and I was rocking mauve Akademiks terrycloth sweats when he walked up to me and said, "You are so beautiful. You should come to my show tonight. I would really appreciate it if you were there."

We kept in touch and dated sporadically, but nothing major came of it. Anywho, the moral of the story is that I manifested this man. He was in my thoughts and I kept watching his videos. This is evidence of just how powerful our thoughts are. Not everyone's imagination may run as wild as mine but what I am here to tell you is that your thoughts do manifest. They may not show up in the same form as I mentioned above but they show up in some form or another.

Those are just a couple of examples of how your thoughts can manifest right before your eyes. This is why it's so important to guard your mind. Your thoughts around money will manifest before you too. Are your thoughts around money centered around abundance or centered around lack? Your current situation, whatever it is, is a result of your thoughts.

Anytime I thought that a bill will get paid, it did. It's just that simple. I have always thought that God would meet my needs and heart's desire and because I hold this belief with such high regard, I find that God always meets my needs.

Your thoughts are so powerful that the Bible even gives you guidance on what to focus on. The Bible says, "Finally, brothers and sisters, whatever is true, whatever is noble, whatever is right, whatever is pure, whatever is lovely, whatever is admirable—if anything is excellent or praiseworthy—think about such things."

Now it's time to seriously meditate and let your imagination run wild. It is so important that you see yourself living the life that you desire to live. Operate from a mental space of already having what it is you want. If it's a certain amount of money in the bank, you need to be able to imagine the money in your account. If you want three maids, a butler, a nanny, and other house staff to manage your home while you work to earn your millions, then you need to first be able to see it. If you want five sports cars, see the cars in your mind first. Maybe what you want is not a material possession. Whether it's a brand new Ferrari or a warm home filled with the love and character of a close-knit family—whatever your heart desires—you must first visualize it in your mind.

Take the next five minutes to pause and imagine your life the way that you desire to see it. Now that you can imagine the life you want, begin to express gratitude for it as if it's already available to you. Allow yourself to be thankful for what you can see, because if you can hold it in your mind, you can hold it in your hand.

One thing you can do that I have found to be quite powerful to shift your thoughts when you are down or in doubt is to keep a gratitude journal. Operating from a space of gratitude is one of the most powerful spaces to operate from. Be sure to keep a daily or weekly log in the journal of the things that took place that day or week that you are grateful for. This is important because you can always go back and reference God's track record. His track record is proven. Tracking the great things that happen in your life allow you to strengthen your faith, and faith, in turn, helps you to reduce your fears. Use the following log to track all the amazing things for which you are grateful.

10 THINGS FOR WHICH I AM GRATEFUL

1)

2)

3)

4)

5)

6)

7)

8)

9)

10)

This practice is easy and will be beneficial if you keep it up in your daily life. Gratitude is the gateway to abundance. So be grateful for what you have and you'll see that life has a way of granting you more.

The combination of gratitude and dreaming creates a powerful force. This is why dreaming is so important. It allows you to imagine bigger and better opportunities and possibilities. When you dream, dream big! God does exceedingly, abundantly above all that we can ask, think, or imagine. God operates in the unimaginable, above what we can imagine. So be sure to go all out. When you dream small, you manifest small outcomes. But when you dream big, the outcome is larger than what you could imagine. Think big, ask big and meditate in this way daily.

As a Christian, I believe someone should be able to look at your life and see God's work. There should be evidence of your belief and God's fruit when an onlooker assesses your life.

Dream bigger and build bigger. God will exceed you at the level of your vision. You want increase in your revenue? Dream bigger!

One day I took a look at my finances. When I saw the revenue, I literally thought, *Wait we have to build bigger*! God supplies all of our needs according to His riches in glory in Christ Jesus. When we increase the need, He increases the revenue. I have seen this happen time and time again. There have been times when my team and I have needed more revenue for our *Fearless Conferences* and the need was supplied.

Chapter 3
The Speech Principle

You shall have what you say

The principles in this book have order for a reason. Now that we have established your belief system, and governed your thoughts, it's time to discuss what you are speaking. What you speak needs to be in alignment with what you believe and what you think. Never allow your mouth to cancel something that you want to happen in your life. All that you speak should be in consistent alignment for that which you want.

There is a saying that we use at the *Fearless Brand* quite often, "Stay on it until it manifests." What that means is that we don't let our hands off of it until we see exactly what it is we have thought, dreamt, and believe to be true. If we say we are getting $50,000 in revenue this week, we stay on it until we see it happen and often until we pass the goal.

All actions and all words must align with your goal. If I say it, I expect it to happen. It doesn't matter what it looks like at all. We stay on it until it manifests whatever the "it" is. Our goal for our *Fearless Marketplace* was to make sure that we had 55 vendors. Once we reached around 30, the team got tired but I reminded them that we had to keep going. We stayed on it until it manifested and we ended up with 58. Not only did we reach our goal, we experienced overflow!

You say you want to pay off your house in five years? Well, you must stick with the idea, visualize the outcome and implement speech that affirms the outcome you desire. Remember, stay on it until it manifests. All of your speech should be in alignment with that goal. If you fall off, don't waste time feeling sorry for yourself or coming up with excuses, simply get back up and cancel out any doubt or negative talk that is contrary to your desired outcome. You must speak in the affirmative. All words out of your mouth must match the goal. No words of lack are allowed. All words have to fit the goal.

You shall have what you say!

I started professionally speaking in 2005 simply because people started asking me to speak at their events, and now here we are years later and people still constantly ask me to speak. "Money just cometh." I know in actuality what is happening. When I speak, I am intentional about speaking on certain topics. By doing so, I am activating the law of speech. My speeches are filled with powerful principles and as I continue to recite them out loud, they are continuously manifesting in my life.

I recently spoke at *Woman Evolve*. This conference

is curated to assist women of faith in growing into the women God has called them to be. Sarah Jakes Roberts is the founder of this conference and her tribe is extremely interactive and engaged. I can remember being excited to participate as a speaker at this particular conference. Not only because I admire Sarah Jakes Roberts' work, but because I believe in her mission and how she is truly helping women evolve. If you've ever heard her speak then most likely you share my sentiments.

I arrived in Denver rocking pink hair and a belly full of eagerness. As I offboarded my flight, I was greeted by the warm smiles and electric enthusiasm of my personal concierge and driver. My host's name was Sarah as well. She was a beautiful young lady whose gorgeous skin glowed with exhilaration. Her curly red hair stood out almost as much as her bright and inviting smile. Talk about a great first impression. I had barely walked off of the plane and I was already feeling the high energy of the conference team.

Moved by the positive intensity of my host and driver, I suddenly wanted to go shopping. It was Sarah Jakes Roberts' birthday and I wanted to get her something special. I asked my host if they could take me by the mall and they happily obliged. I was so excited to learn that the mall we were shopping at had a Z Galleria inside. This particular store was special to me because they sell a certain item that I like to purchase for special friends. This particular item holds extreme sentimental value. I wanted to buy it for Sarah and I knew that she would appreciate the significance of the item.

I was having such a great time with my host and driver that I offered to treat them to dinner. Once I had purchased the gift, we left Z Galleria and went to get the gift wrapped. As we were making our way there, I stopped in my tracks and said out loud to my host Sarah and my driver Vashon that we were all going to get a million dollars this weekend. My tone was sure and absolute. They responded with a smile. I love being around people with high energy and high belief. In my experience working with people, I have learned to value both energy and environment. The energy I experienced with both Sarah and Vashon had been so high that I knew I was in an atmosphere in which I could speak and manifest. I was with believers who knew and understood the power of agreement. Great energy is something that I can pick up intuitively. I can't give you any practicalities to identify when you are in the presence of good energy; it's something that you just know, and because I felt it in my spirit, I was compelled to speak and sow seeds in that moment.

You see, what I know for sure is that the words you speak become seeds that sprout and bring forth fruit. The key is speaking good words, sowing good seeds, and then making sure you sow on good ground. Being among believers was my indicator that I was on good ground.

A couple of days later, I had to speak in my break out session. After my session, I began to sell signed copies of my book. The line to get copies of my book was so long that we had to avoid blocking the traffic of women trying to make their way into the next speaker session. I sold out of all of the products I had on hand.

As we began to wrap up, a lady walked up to my table to purchase the very last book. When she opened her wallet to pay for it. She had four one million-dollar faux bills in her hand. She handed one to me, one to my host Sarah, and one to my driver Vashon, and kept the last one for herself. We all looked at one another and burst out laughing. Here we were with the one million dollars each that I had spoken into the universe. As we all giggled in amusement, I said to them both that I should have been more specific. You see, at the mall I told them that we would each receive one million dollars that weekend. What I should have said is that we would all receive a million dollars in our bank accounts.

Just that quickly, the words that I had declared so boldly in faith were already showing up in my physical world. So not only should you speak only what you desire to see, but it's so important that you be specific in what you ask and declare.

That day I was reminded about the power of bold belief and affirmative speech. Back your words with unrelenting belief and speak with authority as if what you say must come to pass. You will be surprised how you begin to attract things into your life.

Life and death are in the power of the tongue, so speak life. Speak life into everything you claim you want. The Bible instructs us to, "Call those things that are not as though they were." One time I spent a week reciting my prayers out loud thanking God for everything in advance. I would say, "God, thank you for life, thank you for my good health, thank you for meeting all of my needs, thank you for providing for me exceedingly and abundantly."

This speech principle is serious business. Make it a habit to speak in the affirmative. Don't say what you don't want, instead say what you do want with boldness, authority and big belief. Don't say you don't want to be broke, remember broke doesn't scare us anyway. Say I AM RICH.

Make sure that your heart and mind are in alignment with what you believe. Whatever your money goals are, practice this. In prayer, thank God for it as if it's already done. Say these prayers out loud daily. Believe that it is yours, speak like it is yours and watch what happens for you!

Chapter 4
The Principle of Sowing

You reap what you sow

The principle of sowing is one of my favorite principles because I actually enjoy being a giver. I always say, "Giving is the best gift that you could ever receive." I love to give! Even in 2004 ,when I was living out of my car, I sowed. I have always submitted to this principle. I sold my clothes to purchase food to eat and put gas in my car. Before that, I tithed and offered from that same money to West Angeles Church of God in Christ. One reason why I didn't deter from this practice was because even then, I maintained a level of confidence regarding money. I knew whatever I was going through at the time was temporary.

I stand rooted in my beliefs even if something doesn't look the way I want it to look. When my reality doesn't link with my beliefs, I know that it's only a matter of time and season. As long as I am fruitful by planting seeds and sowing, I know that I always have a harvest waiting to sprout up at its appointed time. Seed time and harvest time happens naturally, as long as you plant seed and water what you have planted, a harvest is inevitable.

The principle of sowing is just like the law of gravity; it exists whether you like it or not. It has no respect of person or religion. It works for everyone.

I never would have been able to tithe the first million dollars I ever made if I had not tithed my first salary, which was $1.50 per week.

-John D. Rockefeller, Sr.
American Industrialist & Philanthropist

Not everyone needs a new business strategy, some people just need a heart change. God gives seed to the sower!

In 2017, we were getting ready to have our very first big conference and I was filled with excitement. I had just finished speaking at the *Girlboss Rally* hosted by businesswoman Sophia Amaruso and I said to myself, "Arian, it's time to dust off that old event proposal from 2011, and get to work on your conference." I don't know what compelled me to put my dream on hold for six years, but hey, God quickly reminded me of what He put in me and He told me to do it. So, there I was all excited. I got the old proposal out. I started booking the talent, and I called on an event producer. I submitted to the event producer all of my ideas for the conference. The event production company then responded with a quote that was well over $446,000.00. After reviewing the quote, I said, "Who is paying for that?"

I went to my assistant Shevon and said, "Ok,

everything that we have planned is going to cost us $446,000.00." Her response was a shocking, "WHAT!"

I said to her, "Yes, but we are going to do it."

She said, "Okay, I will stand in agreement with you."

It's so important that you have people around you who will believe in you and stand in agreement with you for what you believe in. Faith requires vulnerability when you need to involve other people, so be careful who you choose to stand in agreement with you.

> *Let me drop you a gem:*
> *Your finances will meet you at your mindset.*

When I asked myself, "Who is paying for that," I was unintentionally affirming that I didn't see how I was going to satisfy the nearly $500K event invoice. The moment I shifted my words and said, "We're going to do this. It's already done. The bill is already paid for," the doors began to open. The conference ended up costing us somewhere between $200,000 and $250,000 versus the $446,000 that was originally quoted. The cost savings was not as a result of us eliminating items from our event production list, but rather because resources started to flow to us at little to no cost.

You want to know how?

We sowed our way out of it. When Shevon stood in agreement with me she asked me how we are doing this. I know that she is a woman of faith, so I didn't mind sharing my plans and ideas with her. I said, "We're going to sow our way out of this bill." I kept all of my charity obligations for that fall season and I continued to sow into charities despite my own massive financial need at the time. My church offerings increased, and any opportunity I saw to sow I did and as I did, the doors kept opening for me.

I'd never really done sponsorship procurement before. I did get a few sponsors for an event that I had curated in college, but that's not something that I'd really done in my adult career. Boy, did I learn fast. I simply applied what I already knew and coupled my knowledge with faith and confidence, and it all worked out. We secured major sponsors like Microsoft, Porsche, Facebook and more.

If you do desire more information on how to secure sponsors for your brand or event, I have actually taught a class on the subject and you can find it at fearlessbrand.co.

On November 18, the opening night of the conference, while standing in the foyer to the large ballroom of the W Hotel in Midtown Atlanta, I looked at Shevon and said, "Girl, can you believe we did it?"

She said, "It's here, we are having a conference!"

We didn't know all of the specifics of how things would work out in the beginning, but that is the essence of having a *Fearless Money Mindset*. We didn't know exactly how we would get the money needed to satisfy the budget for the conference, but we knew that the end would be a victory. We applied all the principles that you will read about in this book and that was the result.

In the principle of sowing and reaping, you know the harvest is coming but you don't always know where it's coming from. Sometimes it comes from the place you sowed and sometimes it comes from somewhere else.

In the days of my PR and marketing business, I sowed heavily into Bishop T. D. Jakes' ministry. I still had my own home church, but I started sowing there too and next thing I knew, one day I looked up and our client Sony Pictures began assigning my company to Bishop Jakes' movies for PR and marketing services. I laughed and thought, "Wow, I sowed my way into this."

It's okay if the harvest you anticipate and cultivate shows up differently and somewhere other than what you expect. Just know this: if you have seed in the ground, it is going to show up. A generous soul will always have; a person who operates in an abundant mindset will always have plenty.

When I found myself in need, I was intentional about giving more than usual. I expected a supernatural increase, and because I understand the principle of sowing, I knew that giving more would allow me to receive more in return.

When it comes to the principle of sowing, if you operate within this principle you will be rewarded as a result thereof. I sold my things just so that I could sow into church because I knew that God was in fact covering me. Time and time again, I noticed that as I gave, I received much more than I could have even imagined. My mother was very instrumental in my allegiance to the principle of sowing, giving back was an ever-present part of my upbringing.

She taught me the value in giving and she always reminded me why it was so important to give from a pure place. When your heart is in the right place, you will always be covered. I learned early on to bless my money as I released it. When I make investments, give back, sow or tithe, I release my money with gratitude, knowing and believing that what I give out is returning to me in abundance.

Harboring negative emotions around money is usually an indicator that you really have deep rooted fears about money you may not even be aware of. Now I'm not telling you to go out and sow all your money unless you feel led to. This is not one of those messages from those TV preachers who tell you to give all your money and run to the mailbox to find a check waiting there for you. That's just foolishness and abuse. Hot mess.com

Though you should always give from a pure place, you should also be responsible with your spending and never reckless. I had to sit my cousin down to have the conversation about responsible spending and sowing at some time ago. She was in high school and had started her own business and began to earn money. When I overheard her ask her mother for twenty dollars to get her nails done, I was confused. Her mother and I both questioned where all of her money had gone. She told us that she had given it all away to the church. Her mom and I explained to her that while doing that is noble, it isn't wise. The lesson here is to sow generously and sow wisely!

Chapter 5
The Action Principle

The secret to getting ahead

is getting started

Woot! Woot! Now it's time to get to work. All your mental mojo is going and you are on fire, but we can't stop there. Action is needed to get anything done. You have to do something. You have to put in the work! You have to have a plan, believe in that plan, and work that plan!

I find that the major cause of inaction is really just fear. People tend to fear the unknown. It's the idea of not knowing exactly how things will play out that keeps most people from making a move. It's the anticipation of obstacles and the perception of difficulty that keeps people from taking action.

What it boils down to is a lack of confidence in one's ability to impact a desired outcome. When you are confident in your abilities, you tend to feel as though you can handle what is ahead of you. But while having confidence is effective, it is hollow when it is not backed with a plan or a strategy. During one of our *Fearless* events, I remember one of our guest speakers teaching on what she called "informed confidence." Informed confidence is the idea of forecasting all possible challenges, working through those perceived hurdles and then creating a course of action to counteract opposition. The key is that when you set a plan in place, you are able to navigate forward in situations that would have otherwise paralyzed you with procrastination or inaction altogether. When you lay out all of the worst-case scenarios and then put a plan in place to remedy the barrier in the event that it actually happens, you can move forward because you already have a master plan.

Having a plan is proven to relieve stress. According to a 2019 survey conducted by the Northwestern Mutual Fund, 44% of Americans report feeling overwhelmed or stressed about money. When I speak with men and women, what I find is that most of their tension regarding money could be relieved with a plan.

The vast majority of individuals succumb to the pressure of bills by allowing feelings of frustration to be their first response. Imagine being $20,000 short on your child's tuition. Instead of getting stressed out or calling around asking for the money, try creating and implementing a plan to earn the money you need. Decide what you have or can offer that is of value. Figure out who will benefit most from what you have to offer. Be intentional about showing up where they are and then be sure to do the numbers.

I can't tell you how many people fail to meet their financial goals all because they fail to take a real look at cost. Whether you are selling e-books or apple pies, you need to be very clear about how much it will cost you to produce it and the quantity in sales required to meet your financial needs. Instead of worrying about how to come up with money, use that time instead to come up with a plan and then keep it moving. In financial crisis or any other difficulty, don't panic, just plan!

Goal setting is such a significant component in planning. Internationally-renowned management consultant Peter Drucker created the Management by Objectives strategic management model in which he introduces the S.M.A.R.T. concept of goal setting. This acronym has become a common and effective guide. Drucker teaches that in order for your goals to be clear and reachable, each one should be:

S: Specific, sensible, simple and significant.

M: Measurable, meaningful & motivating.

A: Achievable & attainable.

R: Relevant, reasonable, realistic & results-based.

T: Time-bound, time-based, time-limited & time-sensitive.

As a rule of thumb, I use the S.M.A.R.T. tool to set goals

and I am always sure to write my goals in the affirmative. So, instead of saying what I want to do or what I hope to do in the future, I write my goals as if they have already taken place. When you set goals, you have to set deadlines and due dates to hold yourself accountable.

Writing out your goals in the affirmative and following it up with inspired action is the fuel that will ignite your vision. While some people don't prescribe to the S.M.A.R.T. goals technique, I have personally found it to be helpful. What I will say is this: if you don't meet a deadline, just adjust it. Don't beat yourself up or get upset. Stay on it until it manifests. If the deadline was for October and you didn't meet it, adjust and keep going. If the goal no longer serves you, adjust and keep going. These tools are put in place to assist you, not to hold you hostage. The main principle is to take action and keep it moving!

Pastor Wanda Martin taught a seminar at our *Fearless Retreat* where she instructed the attendees to write out their top 7-10 goals every day for 21 days. Each day, the key was to write out a list of goals from scratch. If a goal did not make the list on one of the 21 days, because you forgot it, it was a good indicator that the "WHY" attached to that particular goal was not big enough.

In author and motivational speaker Simon Sinek's book *Start With Why,* he highlights how our sense of purpose is the biggest key to success and I couldn't agree more. People don't buy into what you do, they buy WHY you do it. Having a compelling why is the driving force for inspired action. When you are able to attach a sense of purpose or worthiness to your goals, you are less likely to fall into the pits of procrastination and other self-sabotaging behaviors.

How you start anything greatly effects the way in which you finish. This is why having a morning routine is so significant. It sets the tone for your day, allowing you to gain control of your time. It is my personal ritual to start each day from a place of peace and clarity. My number one rule is to not check emails or social media at the top of the morning. After working with several high-profile clients in the music industry, in 2009 I made the decision to remove the email app from my mobile device altogether. When emails filled with client needs and company demands—paired with social scrolling and other digital media shenanigans—consume the beginning of your day, it causes increased stress. The need to respond to the needs of others before you address your personal needs is not only a distraction; it lacks the practice of self-love and appreciation of personal value. As an entrepreneur, I learned very quickly just how necessary it was to dictate my day.

It is a must that I start my day with peace. The very first thing I do is give thanks to God and I sit with my thoughts. I make it a practice to pray, read and meditate on scriptures, and work out before I show up to serve anything or anyone else. I know that when I give myself the care, love, attention and affirmation that I need to operate as my best self, then I can serve others from a full cup. In fact, I make it a habit to keep myself all filled up so that I can serve others from my overflow.

In order to command your morning with self-care, it is wise to wake up early enough to participate in your personally curated morning routine without sacrificing valuable work hours. For those with small children, you may have to wake up even earlier. It is healthy for everyone to mandate time for themselves, even if that means starting your day at 5am or 6am when the rest of your home is fast asleep.

Another adversary to taking action is the presence of distractions. A distraction is anything that is not in alignment with what you are supposed to be doing; it is essentially anything that takes your focus away from your goals. It is so easy to identify distractions when they are obvious and add no value like scrolling on Instagram, or taking the day to go shopping or hanging out at the cigar lounge all day when you have an important deadline to meet. That's obvious and clear. The distractions that get tricky are the distractions that hold value. Just the other day, my father called me on the phone and started to tell me about a very lucrative real estate venture in my hometown of Detroit that he wanted me to be a part of. The spread on the deal was astronomical; it would have definitely been worth my while.

As my father continued sharing the specs on the deal, I responded by letting him know that the deal sounded so good, however it was a good distraction. He understood completely and we ended the call. Now had I said yes to the opportunity, perhaps you wouldn't be holding this book in your hand because it may have been shelved for another opportune time, or maybe my *Fearless Fund* wouldn't have gotten the effort and attention necessary to make sure we get capital in the hands of winning entrepreneurs. The truth of the matter is that even some really good opportunities are distractions because they take time, attention and focus away from your purposeful goals. Distractions, whether they are good, bad, big or small, take you off course.

Being able to first identify distractions and recognize potential distractions helps you to decline them with grace and ease. To recap:

1. **Informed Confidence Plan**
2. **Smart Goals Plan**
3. **Identify Your Why**
4. **Establish Your Morning Routine**
5. **Eliminate Distractions**

After you've done all that, make sure of one thing: do not overdo it. If you are like me, you have a serious work ethic! In the recent surge of empowerment and entrepreneur movements, we've heard a lot about the law of attraction and the law of assertion. The law of attraction is the belief that positive or negative thoughts bring positive or negative experiences into a person's life. Conversely, instead of attracting things through vibration and frequency, the law of assertion is where you actually perform an act.

You want to put in the work because action is needed. Though action is required, don't over obsess. Instead, find the rhythm of putting in the work and allowing things to come to you as well. Things are actually coming to you because you are working. But don't overdo it and miss out on the magic. Don't be a control freak, do the work, activate your faith, and leave room for God to perform miracles.

Chapter 6
The Relationship Principle

Relationships are currency

Cultivating relationships is a lesson in managing people and mastering systems. The people with whom you are connected should bring value in one way or another. That value should flow interchangeably. You should bring value to people as well. Anyone who has encountered you should leave your presence better than before they met you.

Your relationships, when properly nurtured will prove to be your most effective and important form of currency. Currency by definition is a system of money. Money in any form used in circulation is a medium of exchange. Your relationship currency is generated by the investments you make in the people to whom you are connected. Currency is a flow and you have to get into it! Do you know why relationships are currency? Just think of it. To receive money, it has to change hands. There is an exchange, be it from your employer, a contract, a gift, a client, a service, or a sale. However you choose to look at it, there is an exchange taking place. Money simply travels from one hand to the other; that's all that it is doing.

When we think about how we develop relationships in our personal lives, we see that building relationships in your professional lives is very similar. Both require time and communication in order to thrive. It's really hard to relate with someone who you don't spend time with, talk to or connect with. I mean, after all, these are the cornerstones of true connections.

You get close to people through frequency of engagement. We all possess a level of powerful intellect and influence in one way or another but the truth is that none of us use it on people that we don't know. Your ability to advance in life, your business or your career will not be limited by how much someone likes you but it will be limited by whether or not they know you. You will be passed up on opportunities when conversations take place among decision makers and no one knows you. You could be the best in your industry, but if you've failed to connect with those around you, then you're a best kept secret that will continue to get overlooked.

If you've attended any business development workshop then you've heard the age old saying: People do business with those who they know, like and trust. In order to reach your maximum potential, you will need to master the art of building and nurturing relationships.

If you make the right impressions consistently, you will not have to follow up as much. Powerful impressions can go a long way. Memorable people are remembered. You will have relationships that don't require as much maintenance as others because the impression was so strong.

Back in 2018, film producer Will Packer reached out to me and asked if I was available to work on a project. I was a bit taken aback because I hadn't worked on a film since 2013. It had been about five years since my last film project and I honestly thought that chapter of my career was over. During that time in my life, my fulltime focus was on building my *Fearless* brand. Although, the opportunity came outside of my realm of focus at that time, I said yes to Will because of the longstanding business relationship we'd built over the years.

During my first day on set, I recall feeling somewhat out of place and even a little bit out of my element. This was weird to me because I had been extremely successful in film. In fact, it was how I began my career. I didn't know if it was the time between my last project or the timing of the opportunity. What I did know was that something inside of me was stirring for answers. As I went forward with my work, I continued to wonder why this experience felt so different. Had I lost my passion for film? I found myself seeking deeper meaning; why was I here? I was determined to figure out the why.

When I met actress Marsai Martin during her first day on set, she came up to me and expressed how excited she was to work with me. I could tell right away that there was something very special about this young lady. She was someone who the elders would say "had an old soul." She was young but very wise beyond her years. She spoke with a level of clarity, confidence and maturity that was uncommon among others who were also 13 years old. She was only 10 years old when she walked into a meeting with a blazer on to pitch *Little* and from that moment she became the youngest executive producer in Hollywood.

When I got the chance to speak with her mother, I was sure to let her know how much I adored Marsai and how gifted she was. I've worked with talented people many times over, but there was something so beautiful and powerful about Marsai. I often watched her in awe. Once I met her dad, we connected in conversation and he told me that he felt led to share with me how Marsai got started in the acting business.

At the time, they lived in Dallas and decided to take Marsai to get professional photos taken. They called them glamour shots. He went on to tell me how Marsai's great grandmother and her grandfather had both passed away.

Before they transitioned, they both shared messages to Marsai and even foretold the kind of success she was to have.

As I was listening to her father share such a sacred story, I had an epiphany. A light bulb went off in my head and lit my soul on fire—it was my "why" being revealed. It was the answer my soul had been searching for. I hadn't lost my passion for film. I was searching for deeper meaning and I found it that day in a conversation about a young girl who was gifted to make a global impact. I immediately expressed to the family with enthusiasm that I had found my "why." I'm sure they wondered why I had suddenly gotten so excited. When her father asked me what finding my "why" meant, I told him that their journey had been a divine reminder of what walking in faith looks like.

Again, Marsai had pitched the movie *Little* in a power suit when she was ten years old, and her career came about after spending a day taking photos with her family. I can imagine that when they checked into the photography studio that day, they had no idea how that small inspired action would catapult Marsai into her destiny. Hearing her fearless story inspired me to focus more on the possibilities that are activated when we simply show up.

From that day forward, I was drawn to Marsai and her family, and I often spent my down time on set with them. As I began to focus more on possibilities, I had already put into motion what it took to start a venture capital fund and opportunities for women to access more capital. I was intrigued by what I discovered and one day I posted something on my Instagram about the alarming statistic on the amount of venture capital funds that women of color receive. I already knew what I had cooking behind the scenes, but I hadn't spoken about it or shared my plans with anyone yet.

After seeing my post online, Marsai's father Josh gave me a call and inquired about my involvement in the venture capital industry. I was astonished because I had not expressed my plans with anyone at that time.

"Come on, A. I know you're up to something, what is it," he asked. I thought, *Wow, this is weird. How do you know*? After, I shared with him how I was in the process of starting a fund to invest in minority female entrepreneurs, his response blew me away. He told me that he wanted Marsai to be an investor and he asked where he could wire the money? I thought, *OMG, see how quick God moves*. The revelation of "my why" appeared. For those who do not know, the

Fearless Fund is a venture capital fund investing in women-of-color-owned businesses at a pre seed, seed, and series A level.

This is a prime example of how our opportunities to advance come by way of the people we are in relation with and proximity to. When it comes to getting in the flow and understanding the currency of relationships, here are a few things to remember:

1. If you want million-dollar checks, you need to have relationships with people who have more than a million dollars in their bank accounts. People can only give you what they have. Not everyone wants this, but if you do, you have to be in the flow of that exchange.

2. Relationships can provide for you what money can't buy. The right relationships can open doors and offer you things that you would have had to pay for yourself. The right relationship can reduce your $500k bill down to $250k and save you 50%. The right relationship can get you a million-dollar resource at no cost to you at all.

3. Look at who someone hangs out with most

and you can determine their income. People hang around people with similar mindsets. The mindset is key here, you can be around someone who is broke, but you cannot be around someone who has a broke mindset. Why? Because the person who is broke with a rich mindset will not be broke for long. The mindset is the shift. If they have made that shift, their bank account will soon follow. It is not healthy or wise to frequent environments where a lack mindset is dominant. That is not an energy you ever want in your space, unless you are ministering to them to help them—but not at a companion level.

Because relationships are currency, spend them wisely. Sow into them properly and operate in reciprocity. Your relationships should be of equal value, meaning that while you add value, you are just as often in the receiving end of it. I'm talking about relationships with win-win outcomes. You have to win and they have to win as well. If they win and you lose, you aren't doing business with them again. If they lose and you win, they aren't doing business with you again either. This is true in both your personal and professional relationships. Since relationships are currency, you must make sure you are in the flow of reciprocity.

Chapter 7
The Principle of Stewardship

You will be given more according

to your capacity

This law is the most critical of all of the principles discussed in this book. The principle of stewardship will help you earn plenty of money if all the other previously-discussed principles are properly and effectively implemented. Having bold faith, improving your self-talk, sowing, and taking action will all help you to reach your money goals. They will literally help you to get everything you want and many times more than what you can imagine.

While the other principles help you to attract, manifest and activate the gifts and rewards of believing, being and thinking well, stewardship helps you to manage what you make. How unfortunate it would be to do the work required to build just to realize that you lack the fundamental skills to maintain what you've earned.

Managing your money requires discipline, understanding how to make your money work for you, smart investments, and consistency. No matter how much money I earn, I make it a priority to invest time, energy and money into learning more efficient and effective ways to maintain and manage the wealth I generate. Starting out as an entrepreneur in college, I learned the best lessons in business through hands-on experience.

Life taught me stewardship. I have always known how to increase revenue, but managing my money and having a sense of financial mindfulness were lessons I learned through trial and error. In fact, every failure, setback or disappointment I've ever experienced taught me something that made me better. In 2013, right after moving to Atlanta,/; I received notice that I was being audited by the IRS. They were auditing me for over $300,000 in what they thought were misclassified funds. I literally fell to the floor in tears. I called my mother and asked how could this happen to me. I asked the IRS and accounting professionals what triggered the audit. Turns out that the amount of my charitable giving —in relation to what I could actually write off— is what triggered it.

Uncle Sam scrutinized my financial records over the course of nine months. Though the audit got resolved, the process of proving my filing legitimacy was inconvenient and also very frustrating at times. Luckily, I had always kept good records, receipts and other documents to substantiate my financial affairs. I still had to pay them a chunk of cash, but hey—I knew this too shall pass. After enduring that long tedious process, I knew right away that I never wanted to experience that situation again.

During the start of the audit, I decided to switch accountants. The accountant with whom I'd previously worked had done my taxes since I had my clothing store. This particular accountant was highly recommended within my social circles and was a good fit for that season of my business. But as my industry changed, my company expanded and we brought in more money, it became necessary to hire someone who specialized in accounting for my particular area of work.

Outside of hiring tax and accounting professionals to advise me with their expertise, I also realized just how key it was to be decisive. People often fail in business when they make critical decisions based on emotion instead of logic. I can't tell you how many people compromise their business by employing staff and team members who are not a good fit, or have proven that they are more of a liability to the company rather than an asset. If you asked most of them why they have failed to fire non-productive or company-compromising staff, they will be likely to tell you that they don't have time to hire and train a replacement. They feel as though it's easier to stick with what they have even though their employee may be performing poorly. Some entrepreneurs hang on to bad staff because they may like their employee as a person and they allow the idea of ruining their personal relationship with the individual to keep them connected in business.

If your finances are suffering, your company culture or brand promise is being compromised, or the employee is simply no longer a good fit, do everyone a favor and fire fast. Holding on is unfair to everyone, including the person you may be releasing from their roles and responsibilities in the company. Business thrives off of great relationship practices, but wisdom, logic and instinct can't be ignored. When it comes to team expansion, I have found it best to hire slow and fire fast. In the words of serial entrepreneur Gary Vee, "When you're hiring, you're guessing, but when you're firing you know."

I have found this to be so true. As you're building your team in the beginning, you're still figuring out best practices, learning the most effective processes and even working through your procedures on top of learning more about the type of people that your business requires in order to operate at its most optimal level. However, when firing someone, you are very clear about why they are no longer a good fit. The problem is while some employees are able to recognize this truth very early on, they waste valuable time and even lose money by hanging on longer than necessary.

If you don't fire people who don't bring value to your company, they will eventually fire you. The livelihood of your business is at stake. You wouldn't stick with a brain surgeon who has consistently failed to meet surgery standards simply because he seems nice and you don't want to rock the boat. Why would you allow someone to maintain their position when they are no longer a good fit? You're probably even doing them a favor by letting them go.

Firing someone is never easy, but the consequences associated with holding onto an underperformer are far worse.

-Marla Tabaka
American Business Coach & Strategist

FEARLESS FACT:
Employees are more likely to find happiness and self-worth when they find a job that is more suited for their skill set and abilities.

Stewardship focuses on discipline, decisions, accountability and responsibility. It is the framework that teaches us that we can earn and keep what we prove we can be responsible for. The Bible teaches us that to whom much is given, much is required.

Everything you have right now is a reflection of your capacity. If you were to earn certain amounts of money in this moment, you would not be able to maintain it. Having increase in theory is a blessing, but when you receive it prematurely, or without the adequate management infrastructure, it will feel more like a burden. Honestly, if you exercise all the previous principles, you will see increase, but what is the sense in positioning yourself for more without the proper tools to manage it? Again belief, speech, action and sowing will help you to get to your goal, but stewardship is what keeps you there.

For me, keeping money at first was a struggle and I mean for real. I can attract money like it's nothing, money shows up daily for me. As Catarah said in the intro of the book, "See it happened again." It had to take many bumps in the road for me to start to save money.

The first time I had a real bill, I was in high school. My mother took me to the Honda dealership to get my first car. I had just turned 16 and I was all excited. I had many extra-curricular activities and my mom was also ready for me to drive myself around. We got to the lot and Mom walked over to the previously-owned cars.

"The car I want isn't over there," I said.

"Well what car do you want," Mom asked.

"The cherry red car with the spoiler and rims on it," I answered.

"Where is that one," Mom inquired and I pointed right at the center of the showroom floor.

"You can have it," she laughed.

"Really?!" I exclaimed.

"Yes," she said. "Because you will be paying for it."

Now let me tell you something. I am not a punk so I knew what she was doing. She was telling me that if I want her to pay for the car then her pick was a used car. But if I wanted what I wanted then I would pay for it.

"You're right, Mom," I said with pride. "I am paying for it." I worked two jobs and always paid my car note. What that moment taught me was that I could have whatever I wanted as long as I was willing to pay for it.

This is half good and half I don't know what because

from there I realized I had a love affair with some Italians. No, I am not talking men. I am talking about some Italians. If you haven't figured it out, the Italians I had a love affair with were Prada, Gucci, Fendi, and Versace. I think I had a date with each one daily.

All jokes aside, I grew up in Detroit and my high school years were during the Biggie aka Notorious BIG era. I was best dressed in high school and I wore them all. I was eager to run to the store with my paychecks and go get fly—not run to the bank with my paycheck and put it in my savings account. Want to know what stopped this life? You either surrender by choice or by force. I am not saying don't buy nice things, but it's all in moderation and in proportion to what you are making. When I went to college, I still had those clothes. When I went to Los Angeles, those clothes ended up in the car I was living out of. I sold those clothes to eat and put gas in the car as you read in the beginning of the book. That is what stopped that habit: life! Now had I learned to save and be more disciplined with money before life taught me, I probably wouldn't have had to wait for life to teach me. Life is a serious teacher.

I look back on my old habits and thank God for my lessons. I am so grateful for evolution. My mom did teach me as a toddler to put money in my savings account at the credit union but somewhere through my high school years of earning my own money, I forgot that lesson. Again, life came around and taught me well.

Don't assume your money will know where to go. You need to dictate in advance where it will go; you must have a plan for it. If you don't have a plan for it, it will move to any undirected place and you will look up and wonder what is going on.

Wisdom must be utilized in all things especially matters of money. My grandmother, who worked in the service industry, taught me just how valuable employing wisdom with investing really is. She was a domestic, cleaning homes for rich families back in Detroit while my grandfather worked for Ford Motor Company. As she worked very closely with the wealthy families she served, she paid close to attention to how they handled their money. After witnessing the family meet with their financial advisor, she approached the advisor and told him that she did not have as much money as her counterparts but wanted to put the little she did have wherever they invested their income.

That wise move afforded her the opportunity to put my

mother through college. The most profound lesson I gained from my grandmother's story was to start with what you have. She instilled in me the wisdom of living, investing, buying and purchasing on my level. My grandmother acquired real estate properties, stocks and bonds. Having lived so modestly, my mom was shocked when she got ready to go to school and learned that her parents had acquired so much. I dedicated my first book to my Naunny, my grandmother.

The best way to prepare for retirement is to have a plan. For salaried employees this can be simple, but for entrepreneurs this may look different. It is wise to have some sort of interest-bearing instrument so that if you place your money in a market, it can yield 10-12% in interest just by sitting. The key here, is to put some aside that is able to sit and acquire interest. Yes, the market has ups and downs but you ride the wave over time and it trends upward.

Most people only consider traditional savings and retirement methods because they believe that these are the only feasible options. You'd be surprised at how many people think that a 401K is the only retirement planning option. Again, this goes back to your belief system.

When it comes to securing your financial future, it's not

a matter of having a 401K or other traditional investment accounts, it's about having a plan plus the discipline to delay gratification so that you can put money away for later. That means having a money mindset that empowers you to save not spend.

Traditional retirement accounts that accompany employment tend to reduce the need for financial discipline. Since funds are usually automatically deducted from your paycheck and placed in your designated retirement account, you don't really need to have a whole lot of discipline to put money away. Essentially, it is done for you. When you implement non-traditional retirement planning strategies, financial discipline is a mandate. If you don't intentionally put money away and allow it to grow interest, there will be no money available to you when you decide to retire.

Whether you are on a non-traditional or traditional route, it is key to hire professionals in finance to help you diversify your portfolio and reduce your risk. Whatever amount you desire to have by a certain age can be obtained through common and uncommon routes. Whether you have $1 million in your 401K or $1 million in another type of account, it's still $1 million.

Our *Fearless Conference* finance panel is always a hit; the speakers go over many different options to invest your money. I remember in 2017 when crypto was hot—not to say it won't be again, but at this time it was on fire. My sister Ashley posted on social media two weeks after the event that if you were at the *Fearless Conference* and did what was advised then your money just doubled. I laughed but it was true.

"Now Ashley," I said. "We do not claim in any form or fashion to be financial advisors. The speaker gave that disclaimer from the stage."

"I know," Ashley said. "But Arian look at my account. My money did just double."

"I know," I smiled. "I got in right after you and mine grew as well. Thanks for the testimony."

My best friend Kellie was also at the conference and she loved the panel. She is the friend I ask what stocks to invest in. She knew about Netflix being a good investment back in 2004 when she was in college in an investing class. She along with all the students invested and their money skyrocketed. She told me to get in on the Facebook IPO and still mentions which stocks to get in and when. She watches the market daily.

My sorority sister Erika Blair McGrew is another person I turn to for personal investing picks. She spoke on that panel that my sister and friends loved so much. After the conference, I ran straight to Erika's house and asked her what I needed to buy. One of those buys increased by 1400 percent.

When Erika called me to let me know to take action before my investment dipped, I asked her if what I saw was right. She confirmed that my money should have increased by more than 1000 percent and that it was time to sell. Do these scenarios happen every day? No. But do they happen? Yes. Do I know it all? Heck no. But what I do know is to keep people around me who know more than me on any subject—especially money.

To wrap all this up, I highly suggest getting a great accountant who specializes in your industry, great financial advisors who can show you how to grow money, and a great attorney for your estate planning who can show you how to pass down your legacy and protect it. You need all of the following below:

1. **Savings plan**

2. **Investment plan**

3. **Charitable giving plan**

4. **Spending plan**

5. **Estate plan**

I hope you have enjoyed this journey as much as I have. It's my joy to share!

Bonus Chapter

Co-founders of Legacy or Lose, a Fearless Foundation initiative, share stories about their households' relationships with money.

Catarah and Carlos Coleman

Legacy or Lose Co-Founders

The longer we live, the more prevalent the phrase,"make plans and watch God laugh" becomes in our lives. As was the case with so many of you, the year 2020 was filled with plans to vacation, attend weddings and graduations, host parties with friends and accomplish personal and financial goals we set before the clock struck midnight on January 1. But GOD had a different plan.

On January 12, the message from Pastor Geremy Dixon at Center of Hope in Los Angeles was about Noah. One of the things he said was, "Stop letting your eyes get you in trouble." We should do so because we know that faith is the substance of things not YET seen. He continued by saying that the worst thing we can do when God's promise is on our life is to look around to try to verify what God has said. The enemy uses the absence of physical proof to keep us from trusting in God, Pastor Dixon reminded us.

In Noah's case, God promised rain, but for many years there was nothing and yet Noah still kept his faith. Pastor Dixon also referenced the importance of being in the boat during the great flood. It wasn't enough to be next to the boat or have intensions to be in the boat. To be IN the boat was the only way to survive. Well, 2020 has been our own personal storm, and faith has been our boat.

During this message, we were being prepared to embark on a journey we had no idea would happen. Still God knew and prepared us by delivering the message of faith and knowing that despite any storm, our faith would sustain us.

Enter the storms.

Not long after this sermon, the storms brewed and revealed themselves. We were first hit with an attack on our health. Both Carlos and I were under the weather. We had horrible coughs, headaches and chest congestion. Los was able to fight through it, but I battled respiratory issues from bronchitis to shortness of breath. It was only January and we felt weak and tired. However, we pressed on. As we did our best to rest and heal, we prepared for Carlos' major back surgery which was scheduled for January 15.

Honestly, there was some trepidation. Carlos wasn't sure if surgery was the right decision for his body. However, at this point we'd prayed and claimed complete healing. We realized there was nothing for us to fear and that surgery was just a process we had to grow through. We also believed that God would stop or prevent him from having a surgery if that wasn't in His plan for Carlos.

The day of his surgery, I texted Carlos at 4:40am: "Baby, I love you so much! With every fiber in me! God is here and He's in total control. Release every negative thought and know that your healing is done in His name! I'm so excited to wait on you hand and foot!"

A couple hours later, they prepped him, we prayed and they wheeled him to the surgery room. My heart was at peace. I knew God would protect him and bring him back whole and healed. Faith had been ignited and so I walked across the street to grab coffee with his mom who was in town for the surgery and we began to chat.

Not 15 minutes after we sat down, I received a call from the receptionist to come back to the hospital ASAP. I won't lie; my heart got heavy. What could it possibly be? He'd only been in surgery for 30 minutes, I thought. I got past the fear and fought for my faith to be restored. During that 5-minute walk back to the hospital, my heart rate calmed and I was ready for whatever was to come.

The first thing the doctor said was, "Everything is okay

but we had to stop the surgery." I could've shouted. I'm sure the doctor didn't realize why me and his mom smiled so hard. We knew that God had protected him. From what, we'll never know, but God intervened.

A week later, the surgery was rescheduled, and we were back at the hospital. God has a way of sending confirmation to ease our spirits and trust that He is with us. As Carlos was prepared for surgery a second time, his surgical nurse walked in and she was every bit of Memphis. Carlos and his family are from Memphis and Carlos spent his high school and college years there. The surgical nurse was a manifestation of home and peace. We took this as a sign from God to trust Him and we did. Today we sit in gratitude for complete healing and the team of angels that were already on hand to see us through that phase.

As storms go, the calm always comes before the big one. Enter COVID-19.

We had prepped and planned for Los to be down for a few months. We had insurance coverage in place and money saved to help supplement the loss of income during that time. We felt that we were prepared. Mind you, I retired last year, to go full fledge into my business: Southern Girl Desserts.

Ultimately our faith was tested instantly. The money we'd allotted was not going to be enough to float us through, but thank God we were in the boat. The world shut down around us, my business and our financial footing was affected due to shelter-in-place orders. While everyone around us panicked, hoarded and thought the worst, we were at peace. There's nothing better for your faith than to recall previous storms and know that it was only God who got you through it. Because of those storms, we were able to ignite the power of faith to get us through this one.

As the world was in chaos around us, our hearts were joyous knowing that even through shortages and business closures, God would not leave us and He would provide. We had the audacity to believe that He would not only provide but would have us come out of this storm in a better financial position then when we entered it. For us, there was no other option but to think, walk, talk and act in faith. Just as COVID-19 hit, Carlos was cleared to work. Because he's considered an essential worker, our home hasn't missed a bill since this happened. Not only have we been able to meet the needs of our home—we've been able to bless others who have not been as fortunate. You see, we are currently in an overflow situation during a pandemic. If that isn't God rewarding faith, we don't know what is.

A shift is happening. Not just the physical shift we are witnessing but a spiritual shift. This isn't the first time God has provided—and it won't be the last. We are sure, however, that fear and faith can't coexist. We had to choose and it's up to you to choose each day which mentality you will adopt for your life, for your finances, and for your health. God does not promise us a life without trials and tribulation, but He does offer us the choice to trust him with all of our heart and lean not on our own understanding. At the end of the day, though our eyes could only see shortages, our faith took over so that we could renew our thinking and live a life free of fear.

And this you WILL do as well.

Enitan and Letisha Bereola

Legacy or Lose Co-Founders

My wife Tish and I have both been the breadwinners in our relationship at different times. The term "breadwinner" implies there's a bread-loser. We're a team who makes the bread and plays to win. My wife has never been my secret weapon; she's simply a weapon. She's literally the best partner I've ever had. I wouldn't be able to be this creative or mobile without her. I'm not the genius I'm credited for being without my wife clearing the way for me to think, dream, envision and fail my way to success. If anyone considers me a G.O.A.T. — then she's Michael Jordan, Phil Jackson and Scottie Pippen combined. Meanwhile, I'm the ball boy who gets a ring too.

You get rings, and you give rings. When I got down on one knee to present her with a stunningly overpriced ring, I felt accomplished. I entered a new level of manhood as if life was a video game controlled by a curious kid from California. Up, up, down, down — the same directions in which life goes. When it goes up, it goes way up! In our first year of marriage, I made more money than the president of my alma mater and that mattered to me. I made more than both my parents' salaries combined and we lived well growing up. I made more money than I could spend after writing a bestselling book. And the more I got, the more I spent. The more money I spent, the less time I spent at home. The more I traveled, the less my wife and I talked. And nothing in the world is more valuable than conversation.

We fell on hard times, but we managed to continue living in a beautiful home by the water in the hottest real estate market in town. We cut back on spending—like no more Louis Vuitton ashtrays. We did away with decadent door-delivered dinners five days a week, and even stopped Googling "where to buy gold toilet paper."

Yes, I was one click away from ordering golden tissue. It hurt me to type that sentence more than it hurt you to read it.

We fired our maid service and food trucks — cleaned up the guest-room piled with purple Bergdorf bags. We settled on a European summer and a kid-less trip to the Caribbean following our California vacation. We took boat rides in lieu of a yacht. Still, we had no balcony furniture to overlook the sunset from our top floor. We ditched Whole Foods for Trader Joe's. And instead of a G-Wagon, we bought a Nissan. We even got rid of cable. It was a privileged lifestyle change;

our white walls were caving in.

Do you know the difference between potential and ambition? Dust settles, people don't. Potential has an expiration date. Ambition has an expectation date. Expect potential to develop while not allowing anyone to use their potential against you. The potential of man is revealed through the power of a woman, and you don't understand the power of a woman until you've had a real one. Love sees through people and finds their truth. Love says I know exactly who you are, and I want you, still. Love is a relentless force that doesn't care what you offer; it only cares what it offers you. Love is a source of sustenance for itself — therefore love is most powerful when it's reciprocal. Give me what I'm worth and I'm going to give you what you paid for. Women need men to get it. Men need women to give it. We both need each other to figure it out.

A relationship is a chance to make someone see who they truly are by showing them who you truly are. A wise person adjusts. A fool remains. Relationships are supposed to encourage development. Growth is part of our design. Some men make it to six feet, two inches tall and stop growing. Some of us quit growing after 18 years of age. Even short adults shouldn't stop growing. We should never forfeit the chance to learn something dope that adds value to our lives just because we're "grown." Being grown is making the decision to be vulnerable, choosing to be available and being willing to serve. That's what a relationship is. And that's what I did. It happens much quicker going down a mountain than climbing one. It's even more challenging to reach that peak again. But I did. We did.

Discovery is the process of purpose. I didn't find my wife, I discovered her. There's a difference. She was already a mountaintop. She was already taking up space. She was already God's work. She was who she was before I got there. I could only love her or leave her alone. As men, we think we bring the table to the table. We think showing up with bread is a contribution, tithe and offering, but what is your value proposition to her already invaluable life? Why should she stop looking ahead to notice you?

Many men think women expect them to come to the table with everything. Quit convincing yourself everything has to be perfect. Lead from a position of love and abundance, not from fear. She isn't looking for someone to save her — she's accepting an equal to build with. She wants a partner. This isn't charity.

She doesn't desire to be your stay-at-home girlfriend. She doesn't care how much you spend as long as it's time, energy and effort. She wants you to keep her guessing. She just wants something different. She wants someone who is done playing games. She doesn't want to pretend she doesn't like you for the glory of the chase. She doesn't feel like waiting hours before replying to a message to make it seem like you aren't important. She doesn't want to do or say anything to trigger a reaction or make you jealous. She believes in chemistry and energy, but science isn't a sign. I am pro-marriage and pro-money. It's time to move the conversation forward.

Telling women to get out of their feelings and get in their bag isn't motivational. We're normalizing independence and convincing each other we are better off by ourselves. One person doing it all alone isn't a celebration, it's a sacrifice. It's strenuous. It's more stressful than cute. You can be a romantic partner and business partner. That's sexy. Support him and watch his world change. Support her and watch her change the world. I'm the most successful I've ever been because my girlfriend said, "I do." Love is our legacy — and that requires real estate, stock and ownership for our family, the community and the culture. She/he who controls the dollar, controls the decision.

So, what's your decision?

Nicole and Artis Scott

Legacy or Lose Co-Founders

It's amazing how changing your energy and thoughts can change your life. When my husband Artis and I had our "financial talk" to ensure that we were equally yoked, we strictly based our conversation on what was on paper. In premarital talks, we'd discussed money in depth—making sure to cover every question and scenario we could imagine. On the surface, we were on the same page. However, we didn't realize until after we tied the knot that our financial planning and spending were not aligned from a mindset perspective.

After marriage, we realized how we'd based our on individual financial decisions on different emotional reasons. We discovered the need to explore our different money triggers as well as the need to give each other the freedom to heal as we approached life in a partnership. We brought thought processes surrounding money into our marriage based on our childhood and life experiences. We became very intentional on taking time to decode what we really needed, make adjustments, and watch life evolve.

How did we make this transformation happen?

We both came to the conclusion that we are what we eat, read, watch and hear; repetition is energy. Wealth can only multiply in environments where it feels welcomed. As individuals, we needed to transition into having an abundance mindset in addition to adopting a family mindset of being a unit that could carry on generationally. Those that are doing well in life are constantly put into positions that bring more wealth into their lives. There's no such thing as luck.

We knew that we didn't come in this world to fit; we came in this world to add. We decided to build wealth for our last name, for our children, our children's children. We became laser-focused on creating a legacy. Our personal family mantra became "contagious abundance."

We started by creating momentum.

We sat down and defined the traits of having an abundance mindset and what a scarcity mindset looked like. We did this so we could be very clear and intentional with our thoughts, our plans, and our actions. Then we defined our family mission statement and our big "why." Momentum cannot come if you do not have access to opportunities and the ability to make choices—the ability to tap into your wealth sources.

I've learned: "You cannot be the light, if you're worried about your light bill." Money is currency and currency is energy.

We sat down and asked ourselves, "What are we here to be a contribution for?" When we gave that contribution a clear definition, it became non-negotiable. And abundance became a way of being able to fulfill our true purpose on this earth.

Next, we had to define what our abundant life looked like and create a strong plan.

Worrying is praying for things you don't want, and if you give into it then you've chosen victimhood. The universe needs details. What is the money for? How much do you need and for what? We had to create a money plan, one goal at a time. Once we had our son, we had to expand this plan and make it even more detailed yet flexible along the way.

Lastly, we needed to get a better understanding of our money languages.

We both read Gary Chapman's *The Five Love Languages: How to Express Heartfelt Commitment to Your Mate.* We needed to transfer this knowledge over to understanding our money languages. Many couples find it difficult to talk about money with each because they are speaking two different languages.

When it comes to your money habits, you can always course correct. We knew that anything we focused on we would attract more of. We got clear on our current financial situation and our goals. We got clear on the saver (me) and the giver (him) and what emotionally drove these behaviors so that we could practice awareness. We outlined and fine-tuned our specific action steps. And we mapped out our goals from an abundance perspective.

We joined together to raise our money frequency and step into our money flow. Money is a renewable resource. Once we truly committed our mindsets to this thought process, our lives began to align accordingly.

Acknowledgements

I express my gratitude to everyone who has contributed to my life, not just to this book, because it's my life experiences that make any of my books possible.

To the *Fearless Tribe*, you all have been on this journey with me, whether you purchased the first magazine, t-shirt, book or attended an event, you are why we do what we do! You all have allowed me to figure it out, try new things, and explore ways to service you more.

To my family and friends, for your continuous support. I am truly blessed to be born into a loving family and have some pretty awesome friends. You all are always there cheering me on, showing up in large numbers, giving me input, unsolicited and/or solicited (laughing out loud)!

Last but never least, to my Lord and Savior Jesus Christ for this abundant life He has bestowed upon me. There are not enough letters in the alphabet or characters to type that could describe my thanks. I'm forever grateful!

About the Author

Arian Simone is an entrepreneur, investor, international speaker, philanthropist, and best-selling author who has been featured in *Forbes, Cosmopolitan, Essence, Huffington Post, Ebony* and more. Upon graduating college, Arian Simone was laid off from her job and went from living in her apartment to living out of her car. She was without a home of her own for almost a year before she was sought out to do public relations and marketing independently.

Building a successful PR and marketing firm from the ground up, she established great relationships in the entertainment industry with clients such as the Sony Pictures, Universal Pictures, Walt Disney Pictures and others. She is credited with delivering publicity and promotions work on films such as *Ride Along, Limitless, Hancock, Takers, and James Bond 007: Quantum of Solace* just to name a few. She has also serviced clients in the music industry.

Arian has transitioned from working with billion-dollar corporate entertainment clients, to operating the *Fearless Fund,* a venture capital fund focused on investing in women of color-led startup companies. She shares her fearless journey with transparency, humor, and vulnerability all around the world!

Additional
Resources

FEARLESS MONEY MINDSET AFFIRMATIONS

1. When I seize the moment, I reap the benefit of multiplied blessings.

2. I see opportunities and I move on them gracefully.

3. Financial abundance is my birthright.

4. My confidence is richly rewarded.

5. I am proactive in securing my family's legacy.

6. I receive blessings in abundance.

7. What I visualize, I materialize.

8. My focus is on abundance.

9. I act as if it's already done.

10. I am fearless in pursuing my dreams.

11. I succeed spiritually, mentally, financially, emotionally, and physically.

12. I am a cheerful giver.

13. I live an abundant life.

14. I walk in the overflow of blessings.

15. All things work together for my good.

16. I expect the miraculous.

17. I am focused on my assignment.

18. I am an excellent steward.

19. Money flows to me effortlessly & easily.

20. I take joy in others blessings.

21. I have victory in every area of my life.

22. I rest when I am supposed to rest and I work when I am supposed to work.

23. I seek to operate at the best and highest version of myself.

24. Everything I touch prospers.

25. My priorities are, in order: Faith, Family, Business.

26. I seek counsel and make wise investments.

27. I operate on the level of my vision.

28. I am a solution to someone's problems.

29. I spend my time and energy in areas that are fruitful.

30. I surround myself with those who see my value.

FEARLESS
PROGRAMS

Fearless Entrepreneur Exposure Program

The *Fearless Entrepreneur Exposure Program* is designed with you in mind. Our goal is to help entrepreneurs, creatives, and authors maximize their exposure by giving access to our community and by leveraging the *Fearless* brand. This program will help you level up, increase your access to a broader audience, and build a supportive network of fellow entrepreneurs.

Program benefits include:

- Monthly video post on our IG stories.
- Monthly post on our IG page.
- Monthly 30-min coaching calls with Arian Simone.
- More than 700 email addresses from our Fearless Marketplace RSVPs to add to your prospect database.
- A directory of all *Fearless Entrepreneur Exposure Program* participants for networking purposes.
- The opportunity to be selected as a monthly guest on the *Fearless* podcast series.

Program investment:

An upfront payment of $1500 ($300 savings)

or

$150/month
This program is a 12-month commitment

Money Mindset Coaching Program

Our community was established to help you grow to be your best and highest self. We collectively walk together to make sound financial decisions, promote discipline and hold each other accountable to hit our financial goals. We are a supportive network to help everyone in life, business and money.

Program benefits include:

- Monthly coaching meetings with Arian Simone and/or the *Fearless* Team.
- Quarterly special guest teachers.
- Monthly evaluation worksheets.
- Weekly goal check-ins.

Monthly coaching meetings are based on the seven principles of this book and are as follows:

Principle #1 - Belief
We review current fears and how to overcome them.

Principle #2 - Thought
We create a gratitude list for the month.

Principle #3 - Speech
We recite our money affirmations out loud.

Principle #4 - Action
We establish goals to review each month.

Principle #5 - Sowing
We determine our charitable giving for the month.

Principle #6 - Relationships
We determine and cultivate our top five relationships on which to focus our building efforts.

Principle #7 - Stewardship
We focus on savings, retirement, investment and legacy.

Program investment:
$25/month
Opt out available at anytime.

One-on-One Consultation Sessions

30-Minute Purpose Session

In this session, you will:

- Assess your passion, gifts and talents.
- Evaluate your current time-spending habits.
- Identify the audience you serve.
- Develop a schedule that aligns with your purpose.
- Develop a goal plan that aligns with your purpose.

30-Minute Business Strategy

In this session, you will:

- Identify your current business stage.
- Identify and develop practical solutions for any existing gaps.
- Develop growth and marketing strategies.
- Identify key strategic partnerships.
- Establish a goal plan for your business.
- Share resources.

45-Minute Wellness Session

In this session, you will:

- Identify personal obstacles and fears.
- Address your triggers and how to plan around them.
- Develop targeted coping skills.
- Share wellness resources.
- Develop a wellness plan to execute daily.

45-Minute Reducing Anxiety Mindfulness Session

In this session, you will:

- Identify the root causes of your anxious thoughts.
- Understand mindfulness and how to utilize it in your life.
- Learn and practice 2-3 mindfulness exercises to mitigate anxiety.
- Create a thought journal.

45-Minute Course Creation & Learning Session

In this session, you will:

- Organize your expertise into tangible course topics.
- Create a strategy for the right learning format(s) for your audience(s).
- Roadmap to tie your knowledge to your audience's learning points.
- Develop options for hosting and assessing audience satisfaction.

All sessions are provided by the *Fearless Team*.

One-on-One Consultation Session Investment:
$250/session

Group sessions are rendered online.
Please register at www.fearlessbrand.co.

Group Sessions

The *Fearless Team* offers group sessions weekly for community members who are in need of hope, guidance, mentorship and more.

Relational Boundaries as a Strategy of Hope Group

This group meets on Mondays at 7pm EST and was created to provide hope in the midst of crisis.

Coping Skills: Managing Stress & Anxiety Group

Meeting each Wednesday at 7pm EST, this group is designed to give participants tangible coping skills, techniques and resources to help manage their stress and anxiety from day to day.

Entrepreneurship Mentorship Group

On Thursdays at 7PM, this group helps entrepreneurs structure their business goals, network with fellow entrepreneurs, and receive expert advice.

Group Participation Investment:
$50 per person/per group

Group sessions are rendered online with the option to attend as often as desired. Please register at www.fearlessbrand.co.

Lightning Source UK Ltd.
Milton Keynes UK
UKHW040911031020
370944UK00001B/65/J